SAVE THE WORLD

PUBLISHED : JULY 2018 | Amazon Createspace. | www.createspace.com

Being Good

Do one good deed every day -It will boost your self-esteem -

Good people in the world must do more good works -this is the only way we are going to save the world number

Tell a person at every encounter -"thanks" At first they may wonder what the person is talking about -But over time they will recall good deeds done by them

Always be thinking the other person as being more important than you

If Someone is rich, they must be rich in good deeds. This is the only way they are going to make it to heaven

Self-discipline -involves giving up something you enjoy once a week - it could be tea / desserts etc

it is not enough to be loving - you must be tough too

Parents are great

It is not a sin to have "self-doubt"

The heart needs reassurance - you could say something like - "You know what you are doing" [Ie I believe in you]

Being honest - You will not always suffer if you admit to something

Declare Muhammad < Islam > and prophets from the Torch < old testament > as saints

Always express what you truly wish for in life - more dreams come true and your heart grows stronger

A woman's night out on the town h- probably Sunday

If you fight sin long enough you will do great deeds

At the end of every day - list all the positive things that happened that day for yourself others

A very good affirmation is "I am worthy of love"

No matter how many deeds you do - your ego should only be as high as you are

Don't worry in life - you will suffer more but you will be happier

Surrounding a person with the people they love with including pet's - can really make a person feel loved

Hope - if you reach for the sky you won't get off the ground but if you reach for the stars you'll at least get to the sky

A good woman lengthens a man's days

Repeatedly ask Jesus / Muhammad to bless you with ideas

BUSINESS

As a career pursue what you truly want to do - you may not make enough money on it at the start - But in the long run you could earn alot of money on it

Every employee should know the history of the company

Tourists been given tours of the factory - like Waterfront Crystal in Ireland

Unemployed people's organisations allowed to go on protest in the streets

Provide a job reference for youths who attend a youth NGO center for a good while

Cultural showcase of your own ethnic tradition for others to sample

MENTAL ILLNESS

If you suffer from schizophrenia just enjoy life

If you are shy or suffering don't be afraid to complain

Don't hide your feelings - be open about them especially people with a mental illness - if you are depressed let it show

Teach men to cry, something most men find hard to do -there are two ways to do this - one way to Repeatedly yawning which makes your eyes to water the second way is to kneel at your bedside and place the palms of your handdose s over the eyes - and talk to God about what is concerned you Both have the same effect as crying

CHARITIES /NGO'S

Encourage charities and NGO'S to write an open letter to this media /newspapers Encourage them to do this on a regular basis   local newspapers would love this act

Publish your expenditure - how much goes where it is needed

At board meeting of charity - one membyer oft the board - read our a passage from the bible study of Them they all say a well-read prayer

Media profile small charities

Charity shops located in the main street of a town / city

A special merit poster for those who have given large donations

At the end of each year charities advertise all the projectDr s they have worked on over the past year

Refugees / asylum seekers should receive the same level of social welfare as other people

Ireland should stay a neutral country - restrictive countries will only allow in charities from such countries

The church should cooperate with local NGO'S in the quest for greater social justice

Social justice should be at the top priority of every third world NGO

NGO'S setting up offices in other countries

Irish NGO'S / charities should include an education pack for school children

COMMUNITY

Tree planting ceremonies for schools twice a year

An open -day for a community - people can drop into each others house for tea / coffee -parents only - police force present in numbers to ensure security

Create mini-gardens in places where the ground is run-down - the term is urban-guerilla gardens

A display with photos of priests who have come from that community over the last 50 years

Sporting events where parents and children compete together

A peace radio station broadcast with UN podcasts / radio programmes

DYING

One family member should take time off work to be with their dying family member

A short television series on the topic of death and the dying

Don't be afraid to talk to someone who is dying

No last minute decisions - if there is something you are concerned about - wait until you have made it to heaven to deal with

Former basketball player "MAGIC" Johnson stated that in the fight against AIDS "abstinence was the safest sex" and not contraception

Hold the hand of someone who is dying and talk to them gently - they may be unconscious but the communication may still be getting through

Family members should be open in talking with the dying about what they are going trough and the fact that they will die

ELDERLY

Bringing elderly people on tour from their retirement homes / village to a children's playground so they can sit down and watch the children playing - elderly people love to be around young children

Elderly people passing on their marriage rings to their children

Neighbours keeping an eye on elderly neighbours. Invite them into your house for tea / coffee every so often

ENVIRONMENT

Protect whistle -blowers reporting abuses by multinationals of the environment

Exposed multinationals by law are expected to apologies in the media - from its home country for abuses exposed

Every country should deal with it's own toxic waste

Green political parties are usually very small - they should think of amalgamating with a major political party They would get ministerial posts and many of their issues would be addressed

A fictional movie about the end of the world due to the environment

All Christian churches should be carbon-neutral

The UN should name and shame companies that put profit before the environment

FORGIVENESS

You cannot enter heaven with a grudge in your hearts

Practice forgiveness even if you find it hard

Forgiveness for people is found to the bible

The Samaritan's should get involved in training priests

Wish for happy things for your enemies

Encourage those who should forgive to actively do something good for their enemy

Create an apology website

FRIENDSHIP

"Why are you always taking the blame"

Befriend the lonely - I know how hard it is to make a first friend

Be true to yourself when making friends Do not be afraid to say you are religious / an introvert / few friends etc

If you don't have friends and you want to make a first friend - Say "I don't have any friends I am just starting to make friends now

If you have no friends you can talk about friends you have had in the past

Develop pen pals between youth from different ethnic / religious backgrounds

ISLAM | MUSLIM-CHRISTIAN RELATIONS

Appreciate this - muslims are good people - Right now muslims on average are better than Christians

A large poster picture of the Koran in the sitting room with a scripture reading

Ask them [Muslims] about Islam

Assume that they are more religious than you

Affirm good qualities about Muslims

If you want to get in a muslims good books - reach out to them in charity

Visit a mosque - Muslims appreciate this

Give a gift to your host - gift giving is very appreciated in Islam

Apologise for Western flaws - promiscuity / lack of morals / materialism w

Acknowledge to Muslims that thier feelings of hurt are real AND that you want to be friends

Never assume you know what a Muslim believes

To Muslims talk about your family and theirs

MARRIAGE / FUNERALS

Renewal of marriage vows at mass for as many groups as spouse

A corner each for recent funerals / baptisms / weddings with photos and messages from people

Include photos of priests at weddings / baptisms - published in the media The Church should be visible in the media

A day of wearing black at mass - to remember all of those who have died im the community over the last few years -a special mass

You don't always have to have strong emotional feelings for each other in a marriage -most marriage would fall if this were the case

If a marriage is on the rocks one spouse should insist that the other kiss them

MASS

Young children especially teenagers must realise that it is what you put into mass rather than what you get of it that matters most

Street masses where the street is closed off for people on that Street

Teenage masses especially around exam time

Say the rosary at mass

A special ceremony where several priests of the church are present

You can say in confession box that you do not want to talk about your sins to the priest

A large picture poster of Jesus in the sitting room with a scripture reading

Night masses for people where candles are distributed once a month

MEDIA

A peace radio station broadcast with UN podcasts / radio programmes

A list of independent journalists contribute to an online counter-culture website

Keep repeating an issue in the media if you want to bring about change

NUNS

Nuns should be allowed to celebrate mass with a priest - nuns read certain excerpts from scripture

Nuns wearing a uniform to identify them - nuns must be seen on the ground if they are to recruit new members

Nuns setting up houses in poor

in poor neighbourhoods - involving the community in as many activities as possible

Nuns making it a policy that all their families and relatives are practicing their faith - they can pester them on this

Nuns can become involved in charities / NGO'S

Nuns asking Jesus to protect their families

Nuns combating "Gossip" -> A flaw in the church at the moment

Nuns liasing in the world with those who would be described as saints

Nuns can move around from community to community

A woman's group supervised by nuns

Community meetings where priests / nuns etc from that city stand up and say why they chose their career path

PARENTS

Parents should not argue in front of their children

If parents want children to talk to them -> They should get into the habit of being silent in their company in the room where they are present

Parents often have fears and worries -> But the reality is that when an problems arises they'll handle it they always do

Parents have to learn to allow their children to make mistakes

Parents should read books by American author Bill Cosby -> who has written at least one book on parenting and the family

Parents should talk to their children about the programmes they watch on tv

PEACE

An cy that specialises in arranging contacts between notable individuals and officials in politics / media / religion

NGO'S can run for election as political parties / individual -> stay independent of other parties < this should shake up the political scene in conflict zones >

A Congress of small nations < in the world >

The Pope can visit conflict zones

School children -> write about good things they know about people / children from other ethnic groups / positive experiences you have had with people from other ethnic groups you have encountered as a project

POLITICS

Politicians record of attendance in parliament and the number of questions / answers they contributed and what they are

All people should be politically aware of what is going on in the world

Publish a booklet on your political party -> it's past achievements and its goals; with profiles of party members and their contact details

Mid-term; half-way through a government term -> parties should propose their policies to their constituencies

Religious organisations as observers at major political meetings

Major religious leaders should develop a close relationship with political leaders

A larger national parliament

A Congress of small nations on peace / development and social justice

Self-criticism of their own side in politics - people would like this

Admit the truth about personal feelings in political settings -You would be surprised - you will be accepted

PRAYERS

People have to start saying the rosary as a family again

A "prayer book" -each day [teenagers] get them to write out their own prayer. After a while teenagers would build up a whole selection of prayers - from which they can pray at night

Pray everyday even if you don't feel like praying

Prayers should be said around the kitchen table - this is where people are most relaxed

Everyone in these times should pray for an angel to protect them

Do one-liner prayers throughput the day

Prayers of the faithful should remain the same throughout the year. If you are persistent God may grant the requests you seek

Short prayers on billboards in cities

Well known poets should write religious poetry

A "Skype" conversation between priests and other members of their church

PRIESTS

Priests should be where young people congregate in the evenings He should ask them what requests they have - that he should pray for

A biography / auto-biography of well-known priests

Priests going away to a private place where they can get away from it all and spend some time on their way in silence

Priests should be easily recognisable to other people - by such actions as carrying a bible with a cross on it / having rosary beads [large] draped around their knecks

RELIGION

People should < ladies > be encouraged to wear jewellery with the cross on it. The crosses should have a figure of Jesus on the cross - otherwise it is just a fashion statement

Churches should allow observers from other religions to share best practices / strategies / ideas / how they encourage others

The more you choose to know the Lord the more he chooses to reveal himself to you

You should think of heaven throughout your life

SCHOOL / EDUCATION

School children should be encouraged to read books that are biographies / auto-biographie

Every child in a classroom gets a reward for their work. This would encourage all pupils to study more

No school subjects should be compulsory

School counsellors going into a classroom - talk about what they do and generalised examples of the issues they face with students

School children should be encouraged by their parents to read books

Do the fun stuff [subject] / [easy lessons] first and last every day at school

Thete should be several computers with Internet access in each classroom

Children may have a favourite author - parents should buy more books from this author for their children

A book of essays from school children from several schools - the best essay from each class - English language. Provide this annually purchased book for school children in exam years

Religious education for schools needs to be reformed - it should reflect more on the things the church is involved and

SOCIAL JUSTICE

Governments should specialises on a particular form of third world aid. Eg democracy {USA] food etc

Students volunteering as lay apostles / deacons for a set period of time

A dossier of leading indigenous charities in Africa - every country country in the western world should have a copy

If a male politician is elected they may bring their female spouses in as politicians without them having to be elected

NGO'S bring issues of a third world country to the government

Young people going where the issues are happening and giving talks there on those issues - saying we do know about your problems and also care and will try to help

SUFFERING

Re :suffering - do simple repetitive jobs -simple is the key to healing

People who are suffering need space - times to be intimate and times to being alone - let them lead on which they want to choose

It takes courage to endure suffering - it brings out the best in others who are helping

While suffering a person should find one thing in life you really enjoy doing - do this every day

Be assured suffering does end

The mantra is what you truly need you shall receive especially if you are suffering

You would not be happy if life was constant sunshine - we need a bit of both - the sunshine and the rain

If you are a person who has suffered alot - you can cash in your suffering for rewards and requests - for yourself and others

A cross / suffering can make you beautiful

UNIVERSITIES

Universities are the place where young people most give up their faiths. Those who are religious - try to convert one person in their life. They can say "if you have looking for a sign from Jesus - just say - if you are real Jesus - give me a sign - if you want me to pray just tell me"

University can have campuses in other countries - this is a good way for these countries to improve their educational systems

Every university / college should have their own radio station

You should make friends with lecturers

Students creative side should be encouraged by their university

Sit at the front row of a lecture room - this is where solid committed students congregate

YOUTH PARLIAMENT

Youth parliaments can submit proposals voted on by them to the Senior parliament. Their suggestions carry moral force

Different political parties for membership of youth parliament that do not exist at senior parliament

The policy department of a youth parliament can include adults

Members of youth parliament have direct access to the leader of the country

An award fund from youth parliament for notable people in Ireland and the world

The youth parliament can use the senior parliament for meetings

Youth parliament can take on one major project in a year. The official government may provide additional funding

A photo of all members - provide photos of works they have done to the media to raise their profile

FAMILY

You don't have to buy new toys for your children - children are very creative and would happily play with broken toys from older children

Photos are cool especially if they are of family members. Parents should do regular photos. When their children grow up they will love their photos

OTHER IDEAS

Apartment blocks should have a common area on the ground floor; where people in them can congregate and talk to each other - this should be a "building regulation"